D0721213

Malaria will keep killing until we awaker
people everywhere; Conaway's poetry p
*Malaria, Poems* is an amazingly candid book.
 —ARUN GANDHI, President, Gandhi Worldwide Education Institute

A novel approach to an ancient problem, these poems powerfully weave to-
gether the scientific facts of malaria with moving glimpses into its unsettling
human toll.
 —SONIA SHAH, author of *The Fever: How Malaria Has Ruled Humankind
 for 500,000 Years*

Humans have seen themselves at the top of life's pyramid. But as *Malaria, Poems*
reminds us, tiny species like the mosquito can control and threaten human life.
This book of poems can inspire us to redirect our intelligence and creativity in
order to stop the ecological destruction that has spread malaria, and to seek the
collective solutions for eradicating this disease.
 —VANDANA SHIVA, recipient of the Right Livelihood Award and the
 Sydney Peace Prize

Cameron Conaway's *Malaria, Poems* is a moving and powerful feat of the
empathic imagination. Poems such as "Still Born" take us into minds and lives
that most of us barely or rarely think about, and the result is both shocking and
inspiring. Conaway breathes new life into the idea that poetry can be as much
about social justice as aesthetic pleasures and emotional insight.
 —ROMAN KRZNARIC, author of *Empathy: A Handbook for Revolution*

Compassion often lies unawakened when it comes to issues of global health.
*Malaria, Poems* awakens our compassion by bridging the distance that often
exists between malaria and those of us living in Malaria-free countries as well
as the imaginary distance we place between distant others and ourselves. As the
line in the poem "Silence, Anopheles" reminds us: "Each other is ourselves."
 —EMMA SEPPALA, Associate Director, Stanford University's Center for
 Compassion and Altruism Research and Education

# MALARIA

POEMS

# MALARIA

## Cameron Conaway

POEMS

MICHIGAN STATE UNIVERSITY PRESS    *East Lansing*

⊛ The paper used in this publication meets the minimum requirements of ANSI/NISO z39.48-1992 (R 1997) (Permanence of Paper).

Michigan State University Press
East Lansing, Michigan 48823-5245

Printed and bound in the United States of America.

20 19 18 17 16 15 14      1 2 3 4 5 6 7 8 9 10

Library of Congress Control Number: 2014936110
ISBN: 978-1-61186-144-0 (pbk.)
ISBN: 978-1-60917-431-6 (ebook: PDF)
ISBN: 978-1-62895-031-1 (ebook: epub)
ISBN: 978-1-62896-030-3 (ebook: mobi/prc)

Book design by Walton Harris
Cover design by Shaun Allshouse
Cover image of female anopheles mosquito is used with permission of Zwiebel Laboratory, Vanderbilt University.

Michigan State University Press is a member of the Green Press Initiative and is committed to developing and encouraging ecologically responsible publishing practices. For more information about the Green Press Initiative and the use of recycled paper in book publishing, please visit www.greenpressinitiative.org.

Visit Michigan State University Press at www.msupress.org

*For Professor Nick Day, Dr. Phaik Yeong Cheah, and the Mahidol Oxford Tropical Medicine Research Unit*

Rachel Hadas —

May this collection serve you and your Literature & Medicine students well.

— *[signature]*

This day relenting God
Hath placed within my hand
A wondrous thing; and God
be praised. At his command,
Seeking his secret deeds
With tears and toiling breath,
I find thy cunning seeds,
O million-murdering death.
I know this little thing
A myriad men will save.
O death, where is thy sting?
Thy victory, O grave?

—Sir Ronald Ross (1857–1932), on
his discovery of the malaria parasite
in mosquitoes, an act for which he
received the 1902 Nobel Prize in
Physiology or Medicine

# CONTENTS

"Bad air" is the English translation of the Italian neologism *malaria*. One bite from the female *Anopheles* mosquito and the very breath of life is threatened. In the Western world, malaria is a word we speak of perhaps most frequently when planning our summer vacations to exotic destinations. We are privy to medication that prevents infection, keeping us safe from "the world's perfect killer." This is not so for people in other parts of the world. Sir Gustav Nossal, a formidable researcher in the field, points out: "it is unconscionable . . . for people to still be dying from diseases that the developed world conquered fifty years ago."

And it is with curiosity, intelligence, and outright rage that Conaway confronts the plague of malaria across the globe. He dives at the subject matter with stinging poetry, so fierce it penetrates the reader's skin, leaving her dizzy and feverish with the power of taut language, infected with Conaway's outcry against the injustice of "the poor going to war for our / sweet wants."

He is a moral tour guide, taking us into the "tropical theaters of war" where "malaria has killed more men than mortar round." He walks us past the child with cerebral malaria, who cannot lift her arms to hold her baby brother, past the stillborn baby slung over an infected mother's arm, one of 200,000 "birthed treasures" buried every year in Africa. And he prods at my own profession, who in their search for breakthroughs, stay safely locked behind sealed laboratory doors, where too often "miracles aren't." Conaway shows us the horror he has seen that is malaria: "although solutions may be on the other side of the blur, I am far closer to the problems."

These are poems of witness and social injustice, airing corruption along the way. By far the greatest strength in this collection is how Conaway, in every poem, unflinchingly reminds the reader "each other is ourselves."

# MALARIA

## POEMS

## THAT'S CEREBRAL

"That's cerebral,"

the doctor said     and it dispersed

slick through thick air
quiet
barracuda

      shuttling sound     away

from mouth     mutating it to mean.

A compliment   in another place

      here sticks
      here clots
      here a death sentence   this time

      to a tribe full of other times.

There        a strong man

whose great ideas
cannot be said

      a lone umbrella acacia alone.    Here

a girl of ten   confused   why her arms won't raise

when she's asked to raise them
   and her baby brothers.

            A tribe muscled
with dwindling

      where cured malaria leaves
trails like listening.

"Roughly one in ten children will suffer from neurological impairment after cerebral malaria, be it epilepsy, learning disability, changes in behaviour, loss of coordination or impairments to speech. As well as being discomforting physically, these problems can also lead to stigmatisation in the community and can reduce individuals' capacity for work, imposing an additional economic burden."

— Ian Jones, "Neurological Damage from Malaria,"
Wellcome Trust, 12 June 2002

## SILENCE, ANOPHELES

> You should have just asked the mosquito.
> — 14th Dalai Lama

It's risky business needing
(blood)
from others
not for science or even more life
for hellos and goodbyes
and most substances between
but so your kids can exit
while entering and spread
their wings long
after yours dry and carry on
by wind not will.

It's risky business feeding on others,
but we all do
one way or another.

It's risky business needing
when you have nothing,
but life has you and lives
writhe inside you.

Risky to solo into the wild
aisles of forearm hair thicket
for a mad sip,
not quick enough
to snuff the wick of awareness
but too fast for savoring.

A mad sip that makes
you gotcha or gone
and may paint you and yours
and them—*Plasmodium falciparum*—
on the canvas you needed
to taste behind.

It's risky business needing
and then getting
and being too *too*
to know what to do—
too full and carrying
too many to fly.

It's risky business being
the silent messenger
of bad news
when you don't know the bad news
is consuming you, too.

It's not risky business
being the blind black barrel
of pistol or proboscis,
but it is damn risky business being
the pointer or the pointed at.

It's risky business being
born without asking
for a beating heart.
Having and then needing to need
to want until next
or else
and sometimes still or else.

Risky when you're expected to deliver
babies and have no gods to guide
their walk on water
because you did it
long before they or him or her or it
never did.

Risky when you're born
on water and capricious cloudscapes
shape whether sun lets leaves
bleed their liquid shadow blankets
into marshes or mangrove swamps
or hoof prints or rice fields or kingdoms
of ditches.

It's risky business naming and being named
while skewered and viewed
under the skewed microscopic lens
of anthropocentrism
an (not) opheles (profit)
a goddess name, Anopheles,
that translates to mean useless
and sounds beautiful at first
then awful when its insides linger.
*An(ophel)es*, you are only 57% different, no,
you are 43% the same as me, no,
I am, no, we are 43% you, no, we all are
nearly, mostly.

It's risky business leaving
large clues—
a welt and then a dying child slobbering silver
under its mother's croon.

It's risky business being
when you don't
because you have two weeks
or less to do doing.

Risky business killing,
but it depends on who, where, when—
self-sufficient Malawi village in 2014
vs. the legend of Dante & Lord Byron.
Mae Sot or Maine, Rourkela or Leeds.

It's risky business killing
killers that always only want
their kind
of tropical retreat.

It's risky business being
small
profoundly—
the speck of black
sesame or apostrophe
blending in the expanse
of rye or papyrus
and taken
onto allergic tongues.

It's risky business sharing
your body with strangers—
uninvited multiplicities hijacking
what you have
because to them you are what you have.

Risky when all know
your 1 mile per hour,
your under 25 feet high for miles,
your 450 wingbeats per second.

Risky business being you
when some want not to fly
weeks with your wings
but walk days atop them.

Is it riskier business being content
and peacefully going extinct
or not being
content and forever brinking
in the bulbous ends of raindrops
that cling but fatten?

Like raindrops and us, *Anopheles*,
when you fatten, you fall.
History favors the fallen.

To drip
a long life
of falling
before the fall
or to live
a short life
oblivious to it all?

Risky that we exchange
counters—DNA mutations
that make some of us
sometimes
sort of
immune to each other's jabs
though hooks always slip through,
and we send each other stumbling,
always stumbling, always only stumbling.

Changing ourselves changes each other.
Each other is ourselves.

They tell us it's risky business doing
being,
but it is more risky being
doing.
Did you hear all that, *Anopheles*?
How about now?
We're asking. We're good at that.
Does all life listen
at the speed of its growing?
Are we listening too loudly
or too slowly to your silence?

"Human malaria is transmitted only by females of the genus *Anopheles*. Of the
approximately 430 *Anopheles* species, only 30–40 transmit malaria" (Malaria,
Mosquitoes, Centers for Disease Control and Prevention, 8 February 2010).

Pregnant women are "four times more likely to contract and twice as likely to die from malaria than other adults."

— The Challenge, Pregnant Women, Malaria Consortium:
Disease Control, Better Health

"Malaria in pregnancy causes 200,000 still births in Africa."

— title of an article in *Ghana Web*, 12 June 2009

## STILL BORN

As the shadow attaches to her toes,
so the mother slings the still
born over her shoulder until night
when her birthed treasure is buried
with the others under the blankets.
At cock's crow she presses the pink
of his unformed lips to her breast.
Soon the dead will have another
Birthday, and she will tell him stories.
Though skin worked as silk turns
rough as road, she will caress
river rock moss with her bare feet
as she traps fish and recalls the never
there of his black downy hair.
In bed when the cold cat curls
around her like fog, it will be him,
and she will match her breath to his.
Unlike most in these hills, she knows
miracles aren't and will can't, but she
is dreaming deeply and nothing beats
back cold like real or imagined smiles.

"Grip, Coughs, Colds, Bronchitis, Asthma, Consumption, Catarrh, Malaria, Fevers, Chills and Dyspepsia, of whatever form, quickly cured by taking Duffy's Pure Malt Whiskey."

    — advertisement in the *Deseret Evening News*, 1902

## STORE (V.)

There is a store that stands out because it is nearly three years old and because it is made of treated lumber not thatch and because its logo is a photo of a man white as lightning using two hands to choke a human-sized mosquito. The store sells insecticide-treated nets, but it has never sold any because each net costs as much as two years of work, and although the store shows no profit, it stays open and clean and luminescent. A local diplomat comes once a month, whenever fits his schedule, to cut the grass around the store with a shiny red lawnmower and from the looks of it to jingle some of the rust off the old silver latch on the door. When the store first opened, an acting troupe made up of people all white as lightning rolled through and put on a free free free performance for the tribespeople. One of the actors wore angel wings and a giant mosquito head mask with antennae that wobbled and must have wobbled so much before in other performances that duct tape was used to hold them together. This mosquito man went around flapping his arms, and when he touched the other actors they all fell to the floor and convulsed and then came to a still or tried to come to a still, after all they were in the grass and had to itch when bugs crawled on them. There was one who never even came close to convulsing or coming to a still though. He was a man who wore a net over his entire body, and he had a cape with the logo of a man white as lightning using two hands to choke the human-sized mosquito. He didn't run around or run from but he frolicked without a care in the world, and when the mosquito came over and danced around this superman and looked confused and then dove in and made contact with the netted crusader, the mosquito fell and then convulsed and then came to a still and joined all the other people white as lightning who were sprawled all over the field trying to be still but giving in to the itching. The tribespeople laughed and cheered, and some were so happy that tears did not frolic but ran down their cheeks, and when the sun hit their tears just right the clear of the tear burned white as lightning.

"Mosquitoes can rapidly develop resistance to bed nets treated
with insecticide."

— Matt McGrath, "Mosquitoes 'developing resistance to bed nets,'" 2011


"The new type of mosquito, however, does not wait until night-time;
it bites while people are outdoors in the early evening."

— Sanchez Manning, "New mosquito poses greater malaria threat," 2012

## GAME I

They say lives are forgotten not
how children toss pebbles for points
into the chicken wire atop graves.

"*Plasmodium falciparum* is so deadly that our bodies decided it better to risk a 25% probability of a dead child (as sickle cell anemia can cause) than to go unprotected." (Bill Shore, *The Imaginations of Unreasonable Men: Inspiration, Vision, and Purpose in the Quest to End Malaria* [New York: PublicAffairs, 2010], 94).

Ethiopians began using a new maize, Silsa Sidist, because it grows more robustly. "The plant sheds pollen at the same time that mosquitoes lay their eggs. And this particular pollen is perfect food for the larvae." The rate of malaria increased tenfold.

— Lynne Peeples, "Malaria vs. Mankind: Chemicals, Conservation
   and an Ancient Arms Race"

# COUNTERFEIT

> "Third of malaria drugs 'are fake'"
> — title of an article by Michelle Roberts, BBC, 2012

Their five faces fade black
in turns inside the shadow
trail cast by the steady sway
of the single yellow bulb
in the cobwebbed basement.

Two cut the powder and two
clean tubes and one with gun—
to profit with pills on people
is as natural as moon song.
Borrow bright, borrow blues.

My eye fills the floorboard hole,
and I look down on them
making a living by taking
the living left in the dying
and knowing it or knowing not.

There the whirling fan blades
measure the bulb's pulse,
count silhouettes not seconds,
swing night like clock tongue
on artemisinin white sand beaches.

There the young men, boys really,
hired for their inability
to break or take or seize
rights or all over the floors.
Blinking days split like grieving.

Boys, stencil-stashed kids really,
who know not their father or Artemis's
or bow's curve, but the butterfly
and hourglass of arrow's entry wound.
Not yet how time tweaks string.

There the kids, slaves really,
who know not the story beneath
their fingernails or the speed
in their bloodstream: Amphetamine
in Chinese means *Isn't this his*
*fate?* Take them to make them.
There the hate I held as hair
bled through the floorboard hole,
to and fro like a floating feather
of then and then getting caught,
lost in the dust of the cobwebs.

"The leading cause of death on our planet. It's spread by the world's perfect killer."

— Cassandra Franklin Barbajosa, "Malaria: Deadly Menace"

## OKAPI

I know the field of grass
is green, but my eyes

know different knowings.
To them green burns black

and white sun splinters
blades like bad memory

or the legs of the okapi
the students work to draw

from inside their hut.
The teacher carries on

her head a basket of stones,
and gives each student one.

*Your own stone*, she says,
*has all you'll ever need*

*to draw the great animal.*
*Feel its shapes in your hands.*

*See its shadows on the paper.*
*Trace its ridges as a compass.*

*Press it hard and it will give*
*itself until it is no longer.*

I see students tap pencils.
Hear them groan at the task.

But cast in the air's canvas
is the gang-raped teacher

who tells me only that it was
"by more than ten" last week.
Who tells me the choice: stay
home and starve or leave

to fields for food and be raped.
Something about the silence

of a place where wails were.
Something about how violence

seals itself silently within us
and we sometimes carry on.

"The war against infectious disease has been won."
— U.S. Surgeon General William H. Stewart, 1969

## WRAPPED UP, IN

*What's worse?* I asked.
*Fire brighter. Cold wins.*
She drummed words
out between beating
teeth. Body of bone
bundled in the ashes
of her skin then sealed
in the dazzling beads
of needing and sweat.
Her eyes are swathed
in jaundice yellow
but reach like ears
far beyond the bush
to the crushing hum
of the waterfall mask,
a blanket of sound
that hides the way
freezing now has her
heels denting dirt.
*Please try to hold still,*
the doctor whispers.
Warm rag on forehead
like a kiss too brief
and barely too long.
*I am,* she says as *I will.*
Birdsong along the river.
A drum signals dinner.
The waterfall explodes.
Chickens cock-a-doodle.
Children laugh loudly.
*Please stay still.*
She is still.
Children laugh louder.

"Human Malaria Parasite Arose from Gorillas, Not Chimps"
— title of an article in *Scientific American*

## WHAT THE SHOULDER KNOWS

She sat there like tomorrow
was last week as the doctor
spoke of the machine she was
linked to and reliant upon for life.

How the dialysate helps remove
the unwanted, how the heparin
prevents clotting, how the sensor
seeks problems then shuts it down.

She listened softly with her lips,
memorization of the mechanical,
and I wanted to listen only to her
and not to this, but I guess I was

delaying talk of another mission
overseas, how I can't numb out
the limp rigor of fallen comrades,
how I want to dialyze memory

and prevent the clotting of seeing
her like this, how when I turn
to leave, I'll look back only once
so my posterior deltoid takes

in her tears of knowingness,
how when the blinding dust
chokes me up each desert day,
I'm all hers until it dissolves.

"Mosquitoes trapped and preserved in amber [Burmese fossils] suggest that malaria parasites were hijacking the insect's insides to reproduce some 100 million years ago."

— Lynne Peeples, "Malaria vs. Mankind: Chemicals, Conservation and an Ancient Arms Race"

## DIE NEVER ALWAYS

Night shadows swallow day shadows,
but somewhere in this world of place
the muscled music of migration
burns the organs of birds to conserve
the water that elsewhere sparks the language of roofs.
Wild: birds armored by feathers the mosquito pierces near the eyes.
Lab: incapacitated mice are strewn like meat strips on a grill
so the baby skeeters can feed through their netted cages.
Elsewhere and simultaneously a clap for a handicapped
with a clap to kill the mosquito bouncing off bathroom mirrors.
We can't peel shadows from sidewalks
and drape their drippings over black-gummed bums
or the floating plastic bags in animal flight that quiver hard in wind
with peristaltic jerks like proud flags
of self-destruction. We can't compost shadows
like experience composts within us.
Larger than their landing spots make obvious.
More than their wings and thorax.
Like stars they are beyond their manmade metaphoric formlessness.
A bear! A warrior with shield! Everything has an origin.
More than the unseen felt silences between,
a depth ecology unquantifiable.
No ideas but in things
and no thought on ideas but in the things behind. What sporozoites!
What quinine! What radioisotopes!
What ectoplasmic cauldron of matter stirs
the addicts to drag their melting postures
like thought's curious curve
like antennae's curious curve
but not like the spruce limb bent low by clamped snow
kowtowing to blazing white or blazing orange Buddhist monks
or French pressed coffee that mimics like melioidosis the steady drip
of our own choking extracts into microwave safe Howls of Moloch—
safe spaces of mechanized mindscapes, humdrum stabilities
of buttoned desperations that buzz but don't,

that are stuck still
in the center of our own created continuums—
a world of place and barely space
with sting nor sing.
Sciencing boils others to crystalloid cytoplasm.
Some from is in. Some in is from.
Then it's judged by Technotemper who forms the alchemy.
The ear
in earth goes unheeded, and the blue and green bioball
spins us on regardless
of how calm the skin
of our texts or waters or wars. Explaining explains away
and we become more important to we
and not subordinate to the whistling lopsided egg riddled with thorns.
Research can't feel
the sentences larvae speak though we know their dance
and come closer to them and distance—
a white parasol, lungs open,
collapses closed
when we need the sun's needs.
Rays reaching into invisible middles. Banded abdomens. We first move
our sentient selves with the bones of breath exhaled
and twitch go the maxillary palps odorant detectors.
Speak the way voice stumbled on tongues before it scraped pages.
If in the mind of mountain we are as still to it as it to us
who left then to listen
to how the portrait of a man as a young
pupa pulls? Directly as the crow or with the long drag
of ribboned scent or wounded cockroach
or the sticky sweet
of the spilled global health money pitcher
pooling along the porous concrete
of male pattern baldness
and obesity and impotence. Why
this is how mosquitoes mate with male head removed! Here here here

is how it injects its saliva so your blood doesn't coagulate,
and here is how the fluid needle proboscis slurps your blood.
Next we move to scent, okay. Yes it sees with wafting
$CO_2$ and lactic acid. People died. People are dying. People are dying?
People are dying! 2.7 million every year. Now. Yeah? What's the
Glasgow Coma Score? What about the flagella?
Who the Nobel?
Seriously. Name the names. Who did what and when and where
on flashcards. Now!
What cauldron of tenure and legacy may stir
the crisp white sails of lab jackets to wake and sleep only after wrinkled
with the dry sweat of loud desperations from
too-damn-far-away-to-give-a-shit-reallys.
The screws of the microscope are rusted
red like Kenyan soil
from researcher's sweat.
Magnified red blood cells look like
dried peaches, don't they? Do you see the dried peaches?
The pictures of yellow veins because parasites devoured hemoglobin
or 30-second celebritized commercials with pop star sounds to malarial
comatose or bloated bellies and cleft lip and palate, but my goodness her
red heels were killer, weren't they?
Commentator swimming through IV to arrest our amygdala and escort
the content of our character, or wallets, rewiring to fill the slugs
of pistol waving hipsters or outsourcing millions of mosquito nets
so tribesman netmakers and those they employed
and those the employed supported
reenter the diagnostic cycle of bulging ribs and oblique muscles that blink
with each breath
and drawn yellow eyes of distrust
in the un or intentional
feeding on weaker to advance with holy cross wrapping paper
strewn on vehicles or business cards or hats or unpromisables.

He even reminds us of Him in these leaf veins. See? Forget the way the
wind's tongue turns green when it speaks through temple bells or the
dead's bloat. These things are things.
And the plastic bags still float.
And the body still wears itself
based on what it's made to do
and what it's done.
And rain thumps tin.
And cicadas thrum again.
The tutoring of darkness will shut down by lights flicked on.
Is the surface of life like the thin skin of stilled
water or the water itself? Is it the brindle of *Anopheles*
or the mosquito being behind
what we've wrapped in name and taped down with distance?
Cranes without necks and wings and heartbeats burst into a plume of
painted white debris.
Blame it. Artify it so blame can lie. See? Blame doesn't die; it sleeps.
Do our bones of breath inhale the animal
as eyes only inhale and never exhale?
Contriving thrives when context dies:
Helixed things aren't born but burnt and set by the licks of combat.
A soundless welding born of bangs and brokens.

"Given the fact that the HIV virus has nine genes and the malaria virus has 5,300 genes, when is their funding going to equal the complexity of the challenge?"

— Bill Shore, *The Imaginations of Unreasonable Men: Inspiration, Vision, and Purpose in the Quest to End Malaria*

# MIRROR

We read
with mirrorlight
how do we say?

Not often enough
to mean
the inverse.

Symbiosis:
see you soon, that's enough,
fear of far with an I

while far with they
stays okay
if it stays away.

We run
as the river lives
through us.

The spur of life
is that we cannot
experience any

entity
in its entirety.

The baby's toenail
or fontanelle.
A sliver of sky
or the crow's eye.

The mirror projects,
we trust
infinite variables:
frontal, quarter profile,
the degrees between.

The other side
is not always,
but there always
is the other side.

Malaria pivots
on the silver
point of poverty.

I is in
the beauty
of the beholder.

"Doctors who specialize in tropical medicine went through the same rigors of medical training and accumulated the same amount of medical-school debt as their colleagues who chose pediatrics, oncology, cardiology, or neurology. But when they chose different diseases, they chose different patients. As a result, they gave up the comforts. . . ."

    — Bill Shore, *The Imaginations of Unreasonable Men: Inspiration,*
    *Vision, and Purpose in the Quest to End Malaria*

# VACCINE

"An effective vaccine has been 5 years around the corner for the
last 50 or 500 years."
— researcher from Cambridge University

The white door has a sensor on the floor that gauges the distance of my
foot and opens, as they tell me, accordingly, and the door shuts airtight
with a hiss, which it also has a sensor for, and just before this they told me
about how vaccine comes from the late 18th century and comes from the
Latin *vaccinus*, from *vacca* or cow, because of the use of the cowpox virus
against smallpox, and then they told me how malaria is a contraction of the
Italian *mala* and *aria*, which means bad air, because people once believed
it was caused by the unwholesome air around swamps, and they told me
to remember that in tropical theaters of war malaria has killed more men
than mortar round. I didn't respond verbally to any of this because my own
senses were distracted as my feet stuck to tape on the floor so they could
be disinfected and a vacuum lowered from the ceiling and swept over my
clothes and hair though my head is shaved. I step through the next door,
and this door I'm told costs fifteen dollars Every. Single. Time. It. Opens
because I have to wear a special astronaut-grade suit that must be imme-
diately thrown away as soon as I exit. I suit up and walk through this door,
and when I hear the hiss of closing I see I am facing a third white door,
and this one has a small double-paneled window like on an airplane, and
I'm told it is military-grade. What's on the other side is blurry, but I see
scientists in white lab coats, and I see the smudge of their many skin colors,
and I see steel dry ice tanks, which I'm told the world's best submarines use,
and then I'm told I can go no further, that this is the absolute limit, that
I'm lucky to get this far because they don't even allow scientists from other
institutions to go this far because they may steal secrets, and then I'm told
that I'm free and, after a pause to clear their throat, that I'm free to watch,
and as the putty shapes move and hand each other things and open things,
I begin to feel trapped, though I'm free to watch, and I begin to feel my own
sensors firing, though they're not military grade, and they're telling me that
although solutions may be on the other side of the blur, I am far closer to
the problems.

"There has never been a vaccine for a parasitic disease."
   — Bill Gates at the Malaria Forum, 2011

"British vaccine breakthrough will save millions from malaria"
   — title of an article in *The Telegraph*, 18 August 2002

"Malaria Vaccine Is Near, U.S. Health Officials Say"
   — title of an article in *The New York Times*, 3 August 1984

## LENS

*lens* (n.) — *late 17th century, from 'lentils' due to shape similarity*

There reaches a focal point
where you can no longer look
at but through the biologic body,
out of the pain of furrowed brows,
out of creased eyes that vacillate
from wince to wild but never slack
and never nothing until a few minutes
after nothing.

Spaces are not voids.

"This is one of the outstanding medical mysteries of mankind. We have perhaps the most devastating disease of humanity, but where it came from has been unclear."

— Nathan Wolfe quoted in "The Origin of Human Malaria"

## IN SEASON

I'm
>in a Starbucks
>in a supermarket
>in a six-story mall
>in Bangkok

alone
>watching        watchers
watch

>a professional fruit basket maker

careful
>labor       a balance
>mangosteen canopy

>in bundled electricity         concentration
>rambutan:

>all red rind ball and yellowing ray
>the sun's son
>a material day
>fraying like we
>flaming white heat in center sweet

to:
>the woman
>>in gator pumps
jostling with the man
>>in silk suit
>>no pleasantries, no eye contact, a throwback dance
>>from
>ages past that is still
>>in     the code
>>in     us
>short steps and shoulder shrugs. She's won.

A tall old foreigner looms behind them
crammed in a black shirt to flaunt
fat rolls for muscle
shakes his head in disgust
lowers levels from      his height
to the Thai wife a third his age
tells her he has and could get better for cheaper.

Never.
I was lucky to sink into a chair here.
All spaces are filled with rolls
of durian paste.

There, a man reads the *Bangkok Post*.

There, a waxy American apple.

There, four blonde kids with Thai nanny.

There, waxy Argentinian blueberries.

There three college co-eds in tight white tops
and short black skirts bat their eyes in
handheld mirrors, elbows on a tableful of textbooks.

There, waxy Peruvian plums.

There, a waxy woman, stitched, fresh
from
surgery.
Wounded on lips and nose and in.

There, waxy South African grapes
top each basket, then plastic
covers the whole thing, then a hair dryer
melts the plastic to keep everything from
falling out and in its place.

None of us holding our
burnt Costa Rican coffee sees the from in
these impossible Burmese rattan baskets
or in each other.

Here I've judged
in laptop from California with parts from
Taiwan and China
those closest.
Complained of complainers even though
everything closed has a door outside—
the basket, the apple, us people.

Believe that.
And outside our outsides a male magpie-robin
from Asia or Africa or other bird from anywhere dances
all the same.
Driven from something in
them to puff their feathers, strut for mate, take
a gecko then bathe in the rainwater collected on a tree's leaves.
From there it watches watchers watching
the clouds.

Migrant workers in
dried bamboo huts in
still postcard mountains in
rainy season
know the fruits are best
to pick when the humid air hums with the ripe
husking of mosquito wings cutting sky,
know the rainy season is the sweetest season,
is malaria season, is when the fullest baskets
may weigh heavy with the cruelest emptiness.

It's often this way.
The poor going to war for our
sweet wants
masked as needs.
One storm stops job
to be done.
Two storm from store impatient
without forming story.

Three, let there not be.

We're all staring
at baskets and seeing nothing.

"There are more nurses from Malawi in Manchester than in Malawi, and more Ethiopian doctors in Chicago than Ethiopia."
    — Gladys Kinnock quoted in "Anamorphosis: The Geography of Physicians, and Mortality"

## OFFER

There's a give and take
we all do,
skin to needle,
its own
hollowed body.

The blade of grass
dulled at the tip
like all the others.

Frayed straw sandals
at the doorstep.

The salt-crusted work glove.

The mosquito synchronizes
wingbeats during sex.
Kinetic conversation.

Lungs drink to fire
or to the depth of dance.

Textured thoughts layer
like wings.

The wise tribesman
does not flinch
when cobra's strike lands
short.

The gnarled
fingertips felt
when we made
the offering
of right hands.
Magic or the gauge of experience.

Rough pages taken
for granted as farmer.
Lumps in life take us all
to white margins—
where lies lived blur
to truths,
honed skills blur
to sky.
Where no joy
rises from the steam
of practice,
or the pores
on the shaved head
of the marathoner
in the adjacent village
close to sweat or dirt.

"At first sign of Malaria, take Grove's Tasteless Chill Tonic. A real Malaria medicine. . . . Grove's Tasteless Chill Tonic actually combats Malaria infection in the blood. . . . Buy the large size as it gives you much more for your money."

— advertisement in the *Daytona Beach Morning Journal*, 1939

## I WANT TO GO

I want to go in the moment
before going in. The concrete
wall seems grayed with knowing.

Ear pressed against the grain
hears the cold simmer of silence
then the boom and echo of flood

in throat. Sound chokes me. I go
in to see brown babies breaking
in their voices. Where walls meet,

a young boy plays with shadows
and over and over kisses the static
outline of his mother's pregnant belly.

Her temples show no trace of voice
in veins, and in that moment I go
and somehow come to on all fours.

I reach, dip my hands in what was
a river, now dried to open scabs,
taste the wink of wounds under scars.

Maybe my eyes are closed. Life still
needles through the water, and I run
cupfuls of absence through my fingers.

"Hippocrates documented the distinct stages of the illness; Alexander the Great likely died of it, leading to the unraveling of the Greek Empire. Malaria may have stopped the armies of both Attila the Hun and Genghis Khan."

— Michael Finkel, "Stopping a Global Killer"

## DENSITY SLANT

(1)

On these rusted roads
are so many people
there are no people,
only one watered wave
of rolling rickshaw
and feet b-boppin'
and rickshaw
and pulse beating birdwing
and colors, so many colors
dulled in the dust of the drum.

(2)

*They find ways*
*to find no way*
*out*, she says.

The rusted red rake
must dig
before it drags.

Easier to muscle a moment
than to move
or make memory.

The must dig
drags before
the rake rusts red.

Tough seeds more
or less bitter
than fear's juice.

The before drags
the must rake
digs red rust.

Easier to ask
the fraud
to bless the crowned

crane, and, when arrow
is airborne,
beg forgiveness again.

The red drags
must dig the rake
before the rust.

A poet works
when looking out
windowpanes—

*So, tell me, how*
*many windows*
*are here?* she says.

Four more gone. Thought:
Has death become an excuse
for celebration?

Infinite prophylaxis will
feed all
who swallow.

The dig before
the rake rusts
must drag red.

Easier to praise
haves who give
than plead needy.

Easier to burn sketches
of secretary birds,
pray it stomps the snake

that killed. Easier
to gift the gone
than give the living.

Five down. Thought:
Has death become an excuse
for art?

Before the red
the rust rake
must drag digs.

Six. Thought:
Has death become an excuse
for business?

Seven. Christ-o-mighty.
Death has become an excuse
for life.

Dense pulses all will
still. Culture can culture
when it's killed.

"Tropical medicine from 1898 to the 1970s was fundamentally imperialistic in its basic assumptions, its methods, its goals, and its priorities."
— John Farley quoted in *Bilharzia: A History of Imperial Tropical Medicine*

## GAME II

Upset safari hunter wanted 60 lbs more.
Natives eat rice and beans and peas
and maybe potatoes from the dirt floor.

"Malaria Helps Syphilis War"
> — title of an article in *The Milwaukee Journal*, 1937

"Jungles 'Safe' Except for Jaguars and Malaria"
> — title of an article in *The Youngstown Daily Vindicator*, 27 January 1938

## LANDSCAPE

> "Malaria is far and away the disease most frequently mentioned
> by Shakespeare, a favorite metaphor for all things wicked."
> — *Politicworm*, "Shakespeare and Medicine"

If I could tell you all the names, it wouldn't be the same, so I'll say my feet sink slightly into the soft soil but not enough that it comes up over my toenails. A blood red ant just carried a twig that must have been three times its own bodyweight on top of and over my foot, and I couldn't move because of the power of it all. My ankles itched this morning, and now they are a bit swollen I guess from bites during the night, and my pants are rolled to below the knee, which is the level of most of the grasses surrounding me ranging from dry and rigid yellow cream to waving ocean algae green, and these are the few who can listen intently and sway to the instructions of Earth maestro. On all sides of me there are huts the size of eyelids, and every now and again I can hear some tinkering or some drum or a cockadoodle. Just beyond these huts hills roll like jaguar shoulders, and where they end blue begins and climbs upward with such organization until an orange sun closes it all up like a navel. To my left there is a puddle, and the rain is coming, and when it does it doesn't play, and it's coming harder now, and the drops pelting the puddle look like a million mosquitos jumping up and down, but this is because they are on my mind and I was born with the luxury to think of them and the malaria they carry as but a metaphor or simile and not as something that could kill me. Even here where I am if I get bit and do get malaria, I'll be okay because of where I come from and who I know and what is already in my system. I am here, but I am not really here as the locals are, and as much as I try I never will be. All I can think about right now as the rain stings my head and my feet sink deeper is how somewhere out there or up there or down there or over there and definitely later on the hush will be accompanied by a hum so gentle as to be imperceptible, and this hum is so gentle that this place is still indefensible against it after all these years of days.

"No more epic struggle between life and death has ever been waged on planet earth."

— Bill Shore, *The Imaginations of Unreasonable Men: Inspiration, Vision, and Purpose in the Quest to End Malaria*

## I. TYPES

"Plasmodium is a tiny, single-celled parasite that infects cells." There are over 120 species of the parasite genus Plasmodium. These five infect humans:

1. *Plasmodium falciparum*: causes the most serious disease; this is the killer.
2. *Plasmodium vivax*: the most common but infections rarely fatal.
3. *Plasmodium ovale*: restricted to West Africa; causes mild illness.
4. *Plasmodium malariae*: isolated and scattered over globe, severe fever, rarely fatal.
5. *Plasmodium knowlesi*: recently discovered in Southeast Asia, potentially fatal. (Wellcome Collection, "The Malaria Parasite at a Glance" and A. Kantele and S. Jokiranta, Plasmodium knowlesi—the fifth species causing human malaria)

## II. HOW IT HAPPENS

"The female *Anopheles* mosquito, hungry for blood, lands on a patch of warm human skin.

"She plants four of her six hairy legs as she dips her head and thorax. She probes with her long, tube-like proboscis, bending back her labium, the lip that sheathes the proboscis. At the end of the proboscis, knife-like stylets move rapidly like electric carving knives to split the skin. She gently jabs at different angles in the hole until she nicks an arteriole that spouts a subcutaneous pool of blood that she can draw from. Exquisitely evolved, the female vampire will squirt into the cut a small amount of saliva full of anticoagulants to prevent the blood from clotting. . . .

"Within a couple minutes, her translucent belly bloats and shifts from waxy gray to cherry red. She sucks a few micrograms of blood—more than her own body weight. Unlike other mosquitoes, the female *Anopheles* doesn't wait until after feeding to start the digestion process. She excretes water from the blood as she feeds. This allows her to pack into her stomach more of the blood's protein while getting rid of what she doesn't need. She lifts in a slow, tottering flight and moves to a nearby vertical surface. There, sluggish from gorging the blood meal, she continues digesting the blood that will provide the nutrients and proteins necessary for her eggs to develop.

"In her blood meal, she has ingested red blood cells, white blood cells, platelets, and other constituents of human blood. And she sucked up something else as well: some protozoan stowaways.

"The mosquito, in a simple act essential for reproduction, ensures the reproduction and spread of another species:" Falciparum.

"The malaria cycle begins once more."

—BRIAN W. SIMPSON, "Putting the Bite on Malaria,"
Johns Hopkins Public Health, 2001

## III. BIO BATTLE I

*Sickle Cell*: "evidence indicating that persons with sickle cell trait are protected against the most serious form of malaria."

—MICHAEL WOODS, "Detection Center Set for Sickle Cell Anemia"

*Thalassemia*: "disease may account for much lower malaria mortality."

—"Decreased Malaria Morbidity in the Tharu People Compared to Sympatric Populations in Nepal"

*G6PD*: "the common African form of G6PD . . . deficiency is associated with a 46–58% reduction in risk of severe malaria"

—"Natural selection of hemi- and heterozygotes for G6PD"

*Duffy*: "The resistance factor to *Plasmodium vivax* in blacks. The Duffy-blood-group genotype, *FyFy*"

—title of an article in *The New England Journal of Medicine*

*Quinine*: Quinine comes from the bark of the cinchona tree. Considered the first effective treatment against *Plasmodium falciparum*, quinine appeared in therapeutics in the seventeenth century. It was the drug of choice until other drugs of the 1940s offered fewer side effects. "Mosquitoes and parasites carrying the disease have developed a *resistance* to *quinine*" *(Fort Worth Star-Telegram)*.

DDT *(dichlorodiphenyltrichloroethane)*: DDT was synthesized in 1874, and its insecticide properties were discovered in 1939. It was found useful in combatting malaria but toxic to animals and environment. Rachel Carson's book *Silent Spring* in 1962 successfully argued against its use, and she has since become heroicized and villianized. "Time is of the essence because DDT resistance has appeared in six or seven years" (PAUL RUSSELL).

*ACTs (Artemisinin-based Combination Therapies)*: ACTs are derived from the Artemisia plant that the Chinese used for over 2,000 years. In the 1960s, *Project 523*, a Chinese malaria research project, rediscovered and improved its use. ACTs remained mostly unknown until an article in 1979 was published in the *Chinese Medical Journal*. ACTs are used to prolong the useful life of antimalarials. The 2010 World Health Organization guidelines consider it recommended treatment for uncomplicated malaria caused by *Plasmodium falciparum*. However, "strains of malaria resistant to Artemisinin . . . are spreading" (Scary Drug-Resistant Malaria Spreading in Asia").

*Chloroquine*: Chloroquine was discovered in 1934, but was considered too toxic for use. During World War II, U.S. government-sponsored trials proved its antimalarial value, and it was introduced in 1947 as a prophylactic. Chloroquine was the most commonly used and most affordable antimalarial. "For 40 years a drug called chloroquine was used as an effective treatment for malaria. But in the mid-80s, African malaria parasites became resistant" ("Malaria drug could 'beat resistance'").

*Mefloquine*: The U.S. Army developed mefloquine for the Vietnam War because of chloroquine resistance. Mefloquine is chemically related to quinine and is completely synthetic. *"Resistance to mefloquine has been confirmed"* (PAUL M. ARGUIN and KATHRINE R. TAN, "Infectious Diseases Related to Travel: Malaria," Centers for Disease Control and Prevention).

*Pyrimethamine-sulfadoxine*: "Over the last 10 years, there have been increasing reports of malaria which is resistant to this treatment" ("Malaria Drug Could 'Beat Resistance'").

Thanks to the following for helping to create, edit,
or feature work from *Malaria: Poems*:

— Wellcome Trust
— International Society for Neglected Tropical Diseases
— Shoklo Malaria Research Unit
— Everhart Museum of Natural History, Science & Art
— Joint International Tropical Medicine Meeting (2012)
— Juxtaposition Global Health Magazine
— Dr. Trent Herdman
— YPSA Malaria Control Program (GFATM)
— Sanaria Lab, malaria vaccine manufacturing facility

ACKNOWLEDGMENTS

CAMERON CONAWAY, executive editor at GoodMenProject.com, was the 2012 Poet-in-Residence at the Mahidol Oxford Tropical Medicine Research Unit in Thailand and the 2007–2009 Poet-in-Residence at the University of Arizona's MFA Creative Writing Program. Conaway is the author of *Caged: Memoirs of a Cage-Fighting Poet* (2011), *Bonemeal: Poems* (2013), and *Until You Make the Shore* (2014). He is on the editorial board at *Slavery Today: A Multidisciplinary Journal of Human Trafficking Solutions*. Conaway's work has appeared in *The Guardian, The Huffington Post, ESPN,* and *Rattle.*

LEAH KAMINSKY is a physician, the poetry editor of *Medical Journal of Australia*, and the editor of *Writer's M.D.*